THIS JOURNAL NOTEBOOK BELONGS TO:

· ·